# A Path to Hope

for Parents of
Aborted Children
and Those Who
Minister to Them

Rev. John J. Dillon

**Resurrection Press**
Mineola, New York

*Nihil obstat:*   Rev. Msgr. John A. Alesandro, S.T.L., J.C.D.
          *Censor librorum*
          May 31, 1990

*Imprimatur:*   Most Reverend John R. McGann, D.D.
          Bishop of Rockville Centre
          June 5, 1990

First published in 1990 by:   Resurrection Press
                P.O. Box 248
                Williston Park, NY 11596

Second Printing February 1991
Third Printing April 1992

Front cover design and photography by Thomas Grasso

ISBN 1-878718-00-2

Library of Congress Catalog Card Number 90-070773

Printed in the United States of America by Faith Printing.

# Dedication

To my parents
who shared with me the breath of life

# Acknowledgements

In gratitude I wish to acknowledge the following who had a direct influence on the accomplishment of this text: Dr. Nancy Benvenga, editor at Resurrection Press, Dr. Robert Kinpoitner, Msgr. Edward Sweeny, Rev. James Lisante, Mr. Luke Tursi and Mrs. Beth Ehlen.

My gratitude is especially extended to those parents of aborted children who have invited me to journey with them on their path to hope.

# Dedication

To my parents

# Acknowledgments

# Contents

In Ramah is heard the sound of moaning,
  of bitter weeping!
Rachel mourns her children,
  she refuses to be consoled
  because her children are no more.

      Thus says the LORD:
Cease your cries of mourning,
  wipe the tears from your eyes.
The sorrow you have shown shall have its reward . . . .

There is hope for your future.

                              *Jeremiah 31: 15-17*


      I know nothing of fetuses,
  but I have known a number of women
      who have had abortions,
  and I am persuaded that almost none
      has been entirely free
      of a wounded memory
          ever since.

                              *Murray Kempton*[1]

# Foreword

In 1986 a young priest approached our office with a concern and an idea. In the one year since his ordination, he'd come face to face with a unique and horrible sorrow. He had struggled to heal a hurt they never taught him about in the seminary.

That caring priest was Father John J. Dillon, and the pain he sought to quell is the affliction of Post-Abortion Syndrome. In the years since then, this incredibly sensitive and insightful minister has journeyed to wholeness with countless victims of this syndrome. His counseling has allowed the broken to hope again in the tenderness and mercy of God. He has helped to create one of the most effective post-abortion ministries in the nation.

John Dillon is a person of striking contrasts. His boundless compassion would be called "liberal" by some. His clarity in naming abortion a grievous wrong might label him a "conservative" to others. He is neither. He is only a faithful instrument of a Lord who binds our wounds and challenges us, simultaneously, to "sin no more."

Father John Dillon helps us to see that abortion destroys life. And he challenges us to recognize that there are always, at least, two victims in every abortion: the baby and its mother, in whose memory the echo of life now gone remains forever.

*A Path to Hope* is a gift for all who seek to be healers and reconcilers. It is a special grace for the hurting seeking the freedom of God's incredible and boundless love.

Father James P. Lisante, Director
Office of Family Ministry
Diocese of Rockville Centre

*Chapter One*

# THE SOUNDS OF WEEPING

## Life After Abortion

"Father, I had an abortion."
"Father, I've held this secret within myself for so long."
"Father, will God ever forgive me?
Can I ever forgive myself?"
"Father, what happened to my baby?"

It is truly an amazing journey being a priest. One is so often invited into the lives of so many people, at times of great joy, times of decision making, times of prayer and reflection. Yet, there is another moment of ministry. A profound moment. When people invite you into their pain; to stand before the cross which they are carrying and pass on to them a message of hope, a word of resurrected life. This has never been as true as when I have encountered those who have shared with me the words written above and many other words of brokenness because of a time in their life which they would give anything to have back. We have termed it "abortion" in our society. But the word does not capture the stories, the people, the tears, and, finally, the new life to which I am a witness. The text which I present to you is intended to be the first word, not the last, with regard to post-abortion reconciliation and healing. My purpose is simply to present some of the essential aspects of this ministry which continues to touch so many lives. My hope and prayer is that you, the reader, might see in these "second victims" of abortion not only the stories of broken and mended people and those who minister to them, but also the face of Christ himself.

The reality of abortion on demand in our country, and especially its legalization in 1973 and the decisions of the Supreme Court in 1989, continue to engender heated debates by those on both sides of the issue. We hear about "women's rights" vs. "the rights of the unborn," "the freedom to choose," "the ability to control one's own body," "forcing one's personal beliefs on another," etc. The argument is often proposed that abortion relieves the stress and anxiety of a sudden, unplanned pregnancy; that it alleviates the pressure, both internal and external, brought about by a conception that was "not wanted." This assertion bears some legitimacy. Many women do, initially, experience some kind of relief after an abortion — not a feeling of joy or gratitude, but usually a response of "having gotten through it," a sense that their guilt, shame or ambivalence about being pregnant is now assuaged. All is forgotten. All is complete. However, many stories of abortion do not end there. In fact, for more and more women and men in our country these stories have just begun.

What we often do not hear about on talk shows, or read about in local magazines, or discuss in classrooms, is the growing number of women and men coming to the forefront and saying, "I'm hurting *because* of my decision to abort." While abortion initially relieves stress and anxiety, it is now being seen as a tremendous *cause* of stress and anxiety: a traumatic experience whose destructive elements remain within the person or persons involved for months, frequently for years. As abortions are

3

currently procured in the millions each year in our country (approximately 1.6 million abortions annually, 4,356 every day, about one every twenty seconds), the cry for healing from those who have experienced abortion becomes more pronounced. So many women in our society, and indeed throughout the world, are suffering the grief and guilt over a lost child who, they now realize, would have been alive if only they had not made this tragic choice.

They are ordinary women and men, bearing no traits that would distinguish them from anyone else. They are young and old, wealthy and poor, faith-filled and non-believers. The painful aftermath of abortion knows no economic boundaries, ethnic lines, religious backgrounds. Ordinary people who work and study, who are married or single, who have responsibilities and times of leisure carry within them an unhealed scar of a previous abortion that is tender to the touch of remembrance. Yet not all those who are hurting have been "ordinary." Gloria Swanson, the glamorous actress of the '30s and '40s and spokesperson for the Year of the Woman in 1976, permeates her entire autobiography with the memory of an abortion which she had at the height of her career. "The greatest regret of my life has always been that I didn't have my baby. . . . Nothing in the whole world is worth a baby. I realized it as soon as it was too late and I never stopped blaming myself."[2]

Patricia Neal, in her autobiography *As I Am*, writes about an abortion which she had many years ago. "For over 30 years, alone in the night, I cried. . . . If I had only one thing to do over in my life, I would have that baby."[3]

Actress Shelley Winters, on *The Donahue Show* a few years ago, was sharing with the audience some of the relationships with men she has had in her life when suddenly she reflected, "You know, I find myself agreeing with the Catholic Church on some issues. You probably will not like me for this. . . ," and she proceeded to tell the audience about two abortions which she had had. "I am a very lonely woman. I would give up everything — my money, my academy awards, my career, if only I could

4

have those children now."[4] Upon sharing her pain and regret, Ms. Winters cried uncontrollably.

These well-known women simply testify to the grief, guilt, regret and brokenness experienced by those who are truly abortion's second victims, the children's parents who go on living. They carry the shattered gift of life in their hearts for many years, many times alone, looking for someone to help them put their lives back together again. Yet even in the popular media we see an occasional hint affirming what so many women and men feel they need to hide. Approximately three years ago I was watching a TV show called *The Bronx Zoo*, which dramatized various events that occur in a local high school in the Bronx. Each episode portrayed the trials and tribulations of teenagers and those who seek to educate and attend to them. This particular episode centered on a running dialogue between a teacher in the school — bright, good-looking, well-respected — and a local priest, concerning whether this particular high school should have a clinic established to hand out contraceptives to the students. The teacher favored the idea; the priest did not. Yet the most poignant and powerful scenes of the show happened at the end. The teacher confided in the priest about an abortion which she had had when she was in high school. In the last scene of the episode, the teacher continued her thoughts with a friend about her experience of abortion. She said:

> "I never knew that I would have such an
> aching sense of loss."

The show ended in silence.

This fictitious teacher articulated beautifully what Ms. Swanson, Neal and Winters have already attested to, and what thousands of women and men are saying about a previous experience of abortion. Their decision to abort has drawn the life out of them, as it violently did to their unborn child. For the mother or father, family member or friend, it is their interior dimension which is so often devastated. It is their spirit which groans and aches to be healed. A child dies and the parents are never the same.

A closer look at that fictitious teacher's statement reveals a world of truth about and insight into those who are dealing with the aftermath of abortion.

- First, "I never knew. . . ." As mentioned previously, the main concern on the part of women who decide to abort is to relieve the stress and anxiety brought about by an unexpected pregnancy. Numbers of women have testified to me that their inner confusion and ambivalence were compounded by those around them who suggested that to abort their child "would be the best thing." Interior confusion coupled with external pressure frequently brings a woman to decide not primarily and consciously to destroy her child but to extinguish the stress associated with the circumstances of the pregnancy. After the abortion there is often — but not always — initial relief. "I got through it," "It's in the past," "Everything is back to normal." What so many were unaware of were the deep feelings of guilt, remorse, grief and emptiness which would begin to plague them as time went on. At the time of their abortion, few women ever thought, or allowed themselves to think, of the devastating consequences to them and their child. "Father, I never knew that I would feel as badly as I do now," is the frequent, anguished cry of parents of aborted children.

- Second, a "sense of loss." Not over "a bunch of cells" or fetal tissue, but over a child that has died a violent death: a person — my son, my daughter whom I will never know. It is so difficult for women to capture fully in words the sense of emptiness which they carry deep within them. Frequently they will attempt to fill this void with things — constant activity, other people, various "escapes." However, the sense of loss over a child never to be known remains.

- Third, an "ache." A sense of loss that doesn't go away: a chronic interior void that jars the heart and conscience. Much like the ache we sometimes feel in our

6

muscles, the ache of the heart takes time to heal, and it will be healed only when it is attended to and worked through despite the difficulty of confronting it. To turn one's eyes away from a wound or scar protects us from the ugliness of its reality, but the wound remains. The wounds and scars of the heart and mind left from an abortion are no different.

From my experience as priest and counselor, I have understood ever more clearly the profound impact that abortion makes on the parents who are its victims. The deep grief and regret which follow in the wake of this event have their origins, I believe, in the fact that an aborted child has not simply *died*, in the passive sense, as though the child had been ill or had died of natural causes. The horrific reality is, rather, that a child *has been killed* and that the abortion was an active event ensuing from a decision made by the child's parents. It seems to me that this is the major cause of the impact of the abortion; this is the horrific truth which so many women and men need to embrace, resolve and be healed of. Fr. James Burtchaell,[5] professor of theology at the University of Notre Dame, takes this premise a bit further by suggesting that the impact of abortion on the parent can be so severe because the action required to destroy the unborn was so small compared to the result. Most abortions are performed in a matter of minutes — so easily, so quickly. For the child's parents, the immensity of the result of the abortion is all out of proportion to the apparent ease with which it was performed. Margaret shared with me that as she was sitting in a local clinic waiting to have her abortion performed, she began speaking to a 17-year-old girl waiting to have her third abortion. Margaret was shocked by this and reprimanded the girl for allowing herself to abort a third time. The girl turned to Margaret and said, "What are you talking about? You're killing your baby too." At that moment, both began to weep.

The professional community has also begun to acknowledge the tragedy of abortion's aftermath. Dr. Anne Speckhard from the University of Minnesota completed a

7

relatively small study on women who had had an abortion 8 to 12 weeks into pregnancy, in other words, the first trimester.[6] The results of her survey are staggering:

85 per cent were surprised at their emotional reaction

65 per cent had suicidal thoughts

31 per cent attempted suicide

81 per cent felt victimized by their abortion; that is, they felt either coerced or that they had not received the proper information

82 per cent felt extremely rushed

81 per cent felt preoccupied with thinking about the aborted child

96 per cent regarded abortion as the taking of a life

92 per cent experienced feelings of depression, anger and guilt

81 per cent stated that abortion led to a severely worsened "self-image"

69 per cent believed that their lives were worse off because of their abortions

46 per cent of all couples in this survey eventually broke up.

Ironically, it is not unusual for women to be unaware that others have had similar reactions. The shame and remorse over an abortion can be so intense that women find it difficult to articulate these feelings or to trust that another will understand them. Patricia was speaking to a close friend about her two abortions and her deep feelings of regret, to which Patricia's friend kept responding, "Oh, don't worry. It was just a bunch of cells." Finally Patricia turned to her friend and said, "Don't you think I miss those babies?" At that, Patricia's friend broke down in tears. She had also had an abortion years before but was afraid to tell anyone of her painful feelings of loss and heartbreak.

Unresolved emotions are a common trait among women and men who are trying to deal with a previous abortion. The death experience itself, along with living in a social environment that doesn't allow them to work through their emotions, often causes them to bury the thoughts and feelings associated with the loss. When the aborted child's parents have no outlet for expressing and resolving their experience of guilt, grief and regret, they must frequently deny or repress these feelings, pushing them down into the caverns of their unconscious and building a defensive wall of psychological and spiritual mechanisms that will try to tame, and protect them from, the ghosts of their past.

However, time begins to break down these defenses. The walls built by denial or repression begin to crumble, brick by brick, as their psyche and spirit ache for healing and wholeness. **Denial** here is best understood as an unconscious psychological mechanism which protects one from some discomforting or unpleasant reality. The reality that needs to be avoided could be an external event or place. For the person who aborts, denial could manifest itself in a number of ways: for instance, in an unwillingness to reflect on or speak about the abortion; or in a repression of emotions or memories associated with the abortion. In 1989 C. Everett Koop, the Surgeon General of the United States, in a letter to the President concerning the after-effects of abortion, cautioned about the difficulty of doing solid studies on women who have had abortions, because denial operates as a coping mechanism in so many. "When compared with the number of abortions performed annually, 50 per cent of women who have had an abortion apparently deny having had one when questioned. . . . It is critical that this problem of 'denial' be dealt with."[7]

## What is Post-Abortion Syndrome?

"Post-Abortion Syndrome" (P.A.S.) is a diagnostic term being used by more and more professionals to describe a wide range of symptoms that are intimately related to, and expressions of, a previous experience of abortion. It is a clinical way to understand what seems to be occurring in those who have directly or indirectly experienced the termination of life of an unborn child. P.A.S. finds its origin in the continual denial, repression or rationalization of thoughts or feelings to the point where these unresolved emotions, which are not being dealt with in a healthy way, begin to exhibit themselves in a number of "symptoms." The symptoms of P.A.S., then, are masks that both express and hide the real difficulty underneath — unresolved guilt, grief, regret and loss.

P.A.S. can be best understood in the context of "Post-Traumatic Stress Disorder," a category found in the textbook of symptomatology used by professional counselors across the country, *The Diagnostic and Statistical Manual (DSM III)*.[8] Post-traumatic stress is a reaction to an event or series of events that are *outside the range of usual human experience*. This is an important consideration. Simply because abortions are done so frequently in our country does not mean that they are "normal" by physical or emotional standards. Rather, abortion is a traumatic event that needs to be recognized, resolved and healed. Following are three causes of post-traumatic stress which are given in *DSM III:*

- serious threat to one's physical integrity
- serious threat or harm to one's children
- seeing another person being killed as a result of physical violence.

Abortion can easily fall into one or more of these categories.

As a trauma, abortion is consistently "relived" in at least one of the following ways:

- recurrent and distressful recollections of the event
- recurrent and distressful dreams of the event
- suddenly acting or feeling as if the trauma were recurring
- physiological distress at exposure to events that symbolize or resemble an aspect of the trauma
- a "psychic numbing" to the outside world which was not present before the trauma.

"The trauma is apparently more severe and longer

lasting when the stressor is of human design," says *DSM III*. With these considerations it is understandable how abortion could produce a physical, emotional and spiritual upheaval in those who have experienced this event in their lives.

Therapist Terry Selby believes that the syndrome begins not with the abortion itself but with the process of decision-making that leads to the abortion. A woman considering abortion frequently has to change her thought patterns, through either denial or rationalization, in order to decide to go through with the abortion.[9] Once the abortion has been procured, the woman must continue to thwart its impact by developing thought or lifestyle patterns that shield her from the emotional trauma: for example, suddenly assuming an extreme "feminist" attitude that was not present before, or proclaiming, "I never wanted children anyway," or possibly being involved with substance abuse or promiscuity as a way to deflect her underlying pain. In 1985 Selby summed up the plight of many post-abortion victims when he said that "attempting to put it out of your mind is what makes you sick."

Certainly, death of any kind can bring about grief, remorse and even guilt. However, while natural death leaves the door open to completion and closure, an abortion is a natural beginning brought to an abrupt end outside of what might be considered the normal course of things. Whenever a natural cycle, such as pregnancy, is begun in a person, and then abruptly and unnaturally stopped (or "aborted"), trauma of some kind is likely to result.

Some professionals have equated the trauma of abortion (Post-Abortion Syndrome) to the trauma experienced by veterans of war (Post-Vietnam or Post-War Syndrome). The same types of stress-related reactions seem to be exhibited in both groups of people:

- experiencing a traumatic event outside of normal boundaries of stress
- unresolved feelings or thoughts (guilt, grief)

11

- symptoms resulting from that which remains unresolved (depression, anger, nightmares, etc.).[10]

Joe was an alcoholic who came to speak to me one day. He had been drinking heavily for some time and simply wished me to listen to him reflect on his life. While thinking back to his younger days, Joe suddenly stopped. His eyes filled with tears and rage. His neck became red and stiff. Joe took his fist and began pounding it on the desk in front of him while crying uncontrollably. "They made me kill Japanese," he shouted. "I was 19 years old. I didn't want to do it. They made me do it. I didn't want to do it!"

Joan was a 30-year-old woman who, at the age of 19, had had an abortion at the urging of her mother and boyfriend. While reflecting on her abortion, Joan suddenly stopped, began crying deeply and pounded the desk in front of her with her fist. "I didn't want to do it," she cried. "They told me I had to. I didn't want to do it."

Joan and Joe shared with me, in somewhat dramatic ways, the unresolved and broken parts of their lives that called out for healing. Though their experiences of trauma were different, they experienced the same kind of pain and grief.

Dr. Julius Fogel, an obstetrician and psychiatrist who has encountered many post-abortion victims, poignantly states:

Every woman—whatever her age, background or sexuality—has a trauma at destroying a pregnancy. A level of humanness is touched. This is a part of her own life. She destroys a pregnancy, she is destroying herself. There is no way it can be innocuous. One is dealing with the life force. . . . You cannot deny that something is being created and that this creation is physically happening. . . . Often the trauma may sink into the unconscious and never surface in the woman's lifetime. But it is not as harmless and casual an event as many in the pro-abortion crowd insist. A psychological price is paid. It may be alienation; it may be a pushing away of human warmth, perhaps a hardening of the maternal instinct. Something happens on the

12

deeper levels of a woman's consciousness when she destroys a pregnancy. I know that as a psychiatrist.[11]

More and more therapists are encountering patients who initially came to them for problems which are supposedly not abortion-related. As therapy continues, it becomes evident that the root cause of a present difficulty is a long-term reaction to a previous abortion. Unresolved conflicts connected to an abortion, hidden at an unconscious level, were giving rise to new problems in their patients' lives. It is only in recognizing their repressed grief and guilt that many women are able to make progress in their emotional health.[12] Antonia entered therapy to try to relieve growing anxiety attacks and bulimia. As therapy progressed, Antonia discovered that an abortion which she had procured about fifteen years before and which she had never discussed with anyone was at the heart of her present difficulties. Once she was able to reconcile herself emotionally and spiritually, Antonia made rapid progress to health.

After more than seventeen years of legalized abortion the Pandora's box is now opened, and all the myths regarding "health," "freedom," "choice" and so forth are flying out. Abortion continues to take violently the lives of countless unborn children, and now more and more people are seeing how it has sucked the life out of the child's parents, grandparents and siblings; in fact, the entire family unit can be affected. Abortion is no longer seen as liberation; rather, it has become a major source of inner enslavement for vast numbers of women and men who so often suffer, for years, in silence.

Yet there is a voice of hope; a voice of healing; a voice of reconciling love for those who suffer abortion's aftermath. It should not be surprising that this voice, this word of hope, is resounding in the Church. The Church has maintained a strong stand on the sanctity of all human life from the moment of conception. Yet it also insists on the immensity of God's forgiveness and mercy. Dioceses throughout the country are establishing post-abortion reconciliation and healing programs that try to reach out to those who are suffering from abortion. Over 60 dioceses around the nation have implemented these programs, entitled "Project Rachel." They are a network of priests, religious and professional counselors specially trained to be instruments of peace and wholeness. It is a way for the Church to say, "We care," "We suffer with you," "We want you to be healed." These programs are founded on the same premise as the pro-life movement: no human life is a mistake. Every human being, no matter what the manner of conception, is a dwelling place for God's Spirit of life. From conception that human being is unique, irreplaceable and sacred. Project Rachel, and programs like it, go beyond this basic pro-life premise and state that the sacredness of the lives of those who aborted must also be maintained. They, too, are precious and irreplaceable in the Lord's eyes even though they might not believe it.

Although the Lord is always ready to forgive, the path to healing for the aborted woman can be a painful journey, one which demands trust and courage. To face the ugliness and truth of our mistakes is never easy for anyone. For the mother of an aborted child, it can be terrifying. Yet as Fr. Michael Mannion, priest and pioneer in post-abortion ministry, has stated, "We cannot be healed of the things we are unwilling to face." It is the dimensions of all our lives which we find too difficult to look at that still remain unresolved and unhealed. For the aborted parent, the process of healing is also coupled with the painful but gentle journey of squarely confronting the tragedy of abortion. The truth of what abortion is can be so painful that many will employ the defense mechanisms of denial, rationalization and repression, simply to try to survive emotionally in their day-to-day lives. However, time begins to break down these walls — weeks, months, years later. Then the unexpressed guilt and grief rise to the surface, and so many women and men do not know where to turn. They can't turn to the father or mother of the child because they might have blotted the event out of their minds. They can't talk to their friends because they might have concurred in the decision to abort. They can't talk to their parents because they either backed the abortion or never knew about it. They can't talk to their priest or minister because "he'd never understand." They can't talk to their God because they think he'd never forgive them. Add to this the fact that we live in a society that has publicly and legally proclaimed abortion as "OK." It has said to the grieving woman, "You don't have to feel bad; you took care of the problem. In fact, you have no right to feel bad. You made the decision." For the parents of an aborted child there is no wake at which to say goodbye; no funeral at which to release their child to God, no body to remember their boy or girl by — simply a date on the calendar. There is no time to grieve — tomorrow's another day. Back to school, back to work, as if nothing had happened the day before.

The 1989 film *Listen to Me* centered around "a story that had never been told publicly about guilt after abortion."[13] Reviewing the film, the movie critic of the *Washington Post* wrote that it "makes you want to say, 'Oh, shut up.' " I wonder how many women and men in our society are crying out, "Listen to me, listen to my regret, remorse and sorrow." Yet these same hurting parents of aborted children live in a society that has said to them, in more ways than one, "Oh, shut up."

Tina came to me at the age of seventeen. A junior in high school, Tina was an intelligent, articulate and beautiful young person. A few months before our conversation Tina had had an abortion. She was too afraid of telling her parents about her pregnancy lest she disappoint them. Her boyfriend thought it best that she have an abortion for which he would pay. Early one Thursday morning Tina aborted her 16-week-old unborn baby. She said to me, "You know, Father, it was terrifying being pregnant and not knowing what to do or who to speak to. It was the worst moment of my life when I had that abortion. But, you know what stays with me now? It was having to go back to school and act as if nothing happened the day before."

Tina had aborted her child. Yet less than 24 hours later she had to walk down her school hall and smile —

just as she always did. She had to sit in class, concentrate and take notes — just as she always did. Tina even had to play basketball on the school team that afternoon and be energetic and enthusiastic — just as she always did. I wonder how many Tinas still remain in our cities, towns and homes who are not only 17 years old but 27, 47, 67, who have never been able to share their guilt and remorse.

In April 1988 *Ms.* magazine published an article entitled "Kathy's Day in Court," which focused on the issue of abortion and parental consent.[14] Kathy was a young teenager, pregnant and wishing to have an abortion, involved in a court hearing trying to determine whether Kathy's parents had a right to know of her wishes. The young girl eventually did abort her child. Yet near the end of the article, there was a hint of what was truly the aftermath of the abortion for Kathy.

> Kathy is tormented with doubts about her abortion months later. "Every time I see something, like if I see something on T.V. about abortion. . . if I see a real tiny baby somewhere I'll think, what did I do? Sometimes I wish I hadn't done it. I don't exactly like the idea of having an abortion. People think you killed a kid, you killed a life. I know I didn't. I didn't!" By now, Kathy is crying. Tears fall, but she doesn't make a sound.

Sadly, Post-Abortion Syndrome is not limited either to any particular age group or to people who have only recently experienced abortion. Many counselors are seeing women and men five to ten years, and more, after the abortion took place. Anne, 80 years of age, had an abortion performed by a midwife sixty years ago. Anne never told anyone of her pain and profound regret. For decades she kept this secret within her mind and heart, trying to forget, trying to repress the feelings, but the memory and the hurt always came back. Finally, one day she read about Project Rachel in a local newspaper. That same afternoon Anne knocked on my door needing to speak to me right away. She had a copy of the article on post-abortion ministry in her hand and, with tears in her eyes, simply said, "Father, this has been the answer to my prayers for sixty years!"

Post-abortion ministry is founded on the premise that women and men who have suffered through abortion have a right to grieve; they have a right to acknowledge and work through their feelings of remorse and guilt. So often they cannot because no one seems to want to listen. Therefore their cry to be healed becomes even more desperate. They seek to be at peace with God, with others who were part of the abortion event, with their unborn child, and finally with themselves. This particular healing ministry humbly wishes to be a vessel of God's reconciling love, to say to those who are broken, "I'm going to be there with you, as a friend. You can be safe here. You can be at home with me." Healing is the ability to offer safety and support for people so that they can go through the process of change. It is being rehabilitated by someone who knows and who cares. It is to have a transformation of heart, a conversion of character, so that we can be freed from the prison in which sin can enslave us.

However, let me make clear that the process of healing can take place only when difficult and painful truths are embraced. Therefore the priest or relatives or layperson ministering to the parents of an aborted child cannot make excuses for what happened. To give the impression of minimizing or disregarding the gravity of this sin would be not only to disregard the death of an innocent child, but also to minimize the guilt, remorse and grief from which these parents are struggling to be freed. At times, out of our own goodness, we can easily fall into this trap. Much like the disciples, we would rather have Jesus go around Jerusalem than face the cross. Yet ultimately it is not what the aborted woman or man truly wants. They have been making excuses for years, using tremendous interior energy to avoid the pain of their cross, and now it's time to stop. To confront the cross can only lead to new life. *But do it gently.* For all of us the discovery of truth can be a difficult, time-consuming process. The process by which memories and feelings are reconciled and resolved can be lengthy, like the laborious process of peeling away

17

layers of an onion. To embrace the truth, however, is the passageway to resurrection. It should never be used as a weapon. One's deep care and concern is one's most precious gift to the aborted parent.

Remember that you are entering a journey of forgiveness and reconciliation with them. Or rather, they have invited you to be the honored guest on their road to new life.

## Notes

1. Murray Kempton, "Dukakis: A Mask of Cold Conviction" in *Newsday*, October 21, 1988.
2. Gloria Swanson, *Swanson on Swanson* (New York: Random House, 1980), p. 519.
3. Patricia Neal, *As I Am* (New York: Simon and Schuster, 1988), p. 134.
4. Quoted in *Catholics United for Life Bulletin*, March, 1982.
5. In his Opening Address to the Healing Visions Conference, University of Notre Dame, 1987.
6. Anne Speckhard, *Psycho-Social Stress Following Abortion* (Kansas City: Sheed and Ward, 1987).
7. Dr. C. Everett Koop, Open Letter to the President of the United States, January 9, 1989.
8. *Diagnostic and Statistical Manual of Mental Disorders* (Washington, D.C.: American Psychiatric Association, 3rd ed., 1987), #309.89.
9. This is particularly true for parents who aborted their child for genetic reasons, i.e. the pre-born child was genetically deformed or handicapped. It must be remembered that, initially, this child was *wanted*. Parents were probably joyful at the news of a pregnancy and looked forward to a new baby. However, as the results of pre-natal tests confirmed the child to be sick or handicapped, pressure to abort (often from doctors, family members and friends) arises. As a result, parents must literally try to erase their thoughts and feelings about their pre-born child to get through an abortion. "My baby" becomes "the fetus," the hope of "birth" gives way to "termination," the anticipation and responsibility of parenting succumbs to abortion "for the child's sake." The anguish that

18

I have witnessed in mothers who aborted children under these circumstances has been especially heartbreaking. Because genetic testing can only be confirmed in the second trimester, many aborted late in the pregnancy. This usually resulted in an abortion through saline injection, going through labor, and giving birth to a dead child. Many women, despite the pressures, had developed deep maternal instincts with their pre-born child — instincts of protection, nurturing and bonding which the abortion destroyed.

10. *DSM III*, loc. cit.
11. Quoted in David C. Reardon, *Aborted Women: Silent No More* (Chicago: Loyola University Press, 1987), p. 141.
12. Anne Saltenberger, *Every Woman Has the Right to Know the Dangers of Legal Abortion* (New Jersey: Air-Plus Enterprises, 1982), p. 154.
13. Douglas Day Stuart, the film's producer, in an interview, Los Angeles, May 25, 1989.
14. *Ms.* Magazine, April, 1988, p. 52.

# Chapter Two

# RACHEL MOURNS HER CHILDREN

## Symptoms of Post-Abortion Syndrome

The trauma and unresolved pain and sorrow over the death of an aborted child affect the child's parents on the deepest of levels. If left unattended, this physical, emotional and spiritual shock will begin to manifest itself in what are now being understood as typical symptoms of Post-Abortion Syndrome. Therefore, P.A.S. (the traumatic impact of abortion) is often *ex*pressed in particular feelings or actions (symptoms) which indicate that the victim has not come to terms with their abortion experience. In other words, if one cannot express feelings of grief, regret and loss in a normal, healthy way, then these emotions must be continually *re*pressed. The persistent pushing down of thoughts and feelings (through denial, rationalization, avoidance, etc.) will often result in these feelings coming out "sideways" — in symptoms of post-abortion trauma. For a person who has aborted to experience any of these symptoms does not mean that he or she is "abnormal" or "crazy." Rather, it reveals that the person's heart and spirit groan to be healed and at peace.

The following are a series of typical symptoms of P.A.S. that women and men from around the country have consistently shared and related to a previous experience of abortion. This is not an exhaustive list. Rather, it will highlight those areas of conflict that seem to be most prevalent. In addition, anecdotal reflections of those who have shared their stories with me will help to illustrate the symptoms indicated. Each story is true; however, the names have been changed to maintain absolute confidentiality.

**Low self-esteem**. The experience of abortion can negatively influence the way women and men view or understand themselves. One's self-concept and self-worth can be devastated when one bears the weight of guilt and remorse over the death of one's child. It is not unusual, however, for this lack of self-esteem to exist before the abortion and to be a major factor contributing to the decision to abort. The comment, "If I'm no good, then neither is the child within me," seems to capture many women's self-understanding at the time of their abortions.

Mandy could not look herself in the mirror after she aborted her child. Her feelings toward herself were so devastating that she was literally afraid to see who she really was in her reflection.

Tara, after writing a synopsis of her life prior to and including her abortion experience, read her reflection to me and proceeded to crumple the pages up and throw them into the waste basket. "I'm not worth a dime," she said.

**Guilt,** chronic or acute. These are feelings of not living up to the standards one sets for oneself, of betraying one's values and conscience. These feelings usually seem to arise when a woman compromises her own true wishes for the wishes of others. Many have expressed the fact that, deep within them, they desired to bring the child to term, but this wish was thwarted by the pressures or attitudes of others. For some women guilt feelings follow

21

the initial feelings of relief which they experienced immediately after their abortion. They cannot understand how they ever could have felt good after destroying their child. As a result, their view of themselves is destroyed.

Josephine initially came to me because of a deep fear about going to confession. When she was a girl a priest told her that she was going to hell for something she had done, and since then she was unable to celebrate the Sacrament of Penance. After I spoke with Josephine for some time, she shared with me that she had had two abortions. Josephine then realized that her fear of confession was mainly due to the fact that she had been racked with deeply repressed guilt for years, and to her conviction that she was going to hell because she had aborted two of her children.

**Depression**, chronic or acute. Post-abortive depression can manifest itself in a variety of ways, including mood swings, lack of energy, lack of interest, frequent crying, inability to make clear decisions or a general somber feeling of dejection.

Loretta would not wash or keep herself looking respectable after her abortion.

Elizabeth went to therapy for a general feeling of depression and unexplained episodes of crying. Only after weeks of professional counseling did she realize that these symptoms were intimately connected with an unresolved abortion experience twelve years earlier.

Joanne was terrified to make decisions in her life because of the fear of the failure which she had felt so profoundly after a decision to abort. Her inability to decide left her dejected and depressed.

**Suicidal thoughts**. Contemplating and/or attempting to take one's life to put an end to the emotional pain, or feeling unworthy to live after taking the life of one's child. It is not unusual for these thoughts to arise around the anniversary date of the abortion or the projected date of the child's birth.

Emily attempted suicide twice. Both attempts took

place during the autumn when recollections of an abortion would tend to intrude on her consciousness. It was during this time of year that Emily aborted her child, as well as gave birth to her only other child.

**Broken relationships**. A tendency to distance oneself from those who were involved or associated with a previous abortion, including the father or mother of the child, family and friends.

Kathy had two abortions. After the first, the father of the child promised Kathy "he'd never put me through that again." When Kathy became pregnant a second time, the father insisted that she have another abortion. When Kathy reminded him of his promise, he simply said to her, "I lied."

Erica was pressured by her family to abort. Her father exhorted her to "bite the bullet" and end her pregnancy in the sixth month. Erica has never been able to speak to her father since.

Marital relationships can also be affected. Bob was Patty's fiance. This couple had aborted a child five years earlier in the first week of November. Bob said that Patty had abruptly broken off their engagement, and it occurred to him that she had done so in the first week of November. In fact, Bob recalled, Patty would always break off their relationship, if even for a brief time, in the first week of November after their shared experience of abortion.

**Nightmares or sleep anxiety**. Dreams that symbolize unresolved issues regarding a previous abortion and which are often horrifying; or the inability to sleep well because of anxiety. Many women hear babies crying in their dreams and cannot find them. Others are stalked by figures who represent their dead child. This symptom is not confined to the parents of aborted children — those who work in the abortion industry are also deeply affected. Nurse Sally Tisdale, reflecting on her work in an abortion clinic, wrote in *Harper's Magazine* in 1988:

I have fetus dreams; we all do here: dreams of abortions one after the other; of buckets of blood splashed on the walls; trees full of crawling fetuses. I dreamed that two men grabbed me and began to drag me away. "Let's do an abortion," they said with a sickening leer, and I began to scream, plunged into a vision of sucking, scraping pain, of being spread and torn by impartial instruments that do only what they are bidden.[1]

**Flashbacks**. Emotionally or physically "reliving" the abortion experience. This is usually actualized by a "trigger event" that sets the flashback into motion. Women have reported flashbacks while giving birth to subsequent children because the same position is taken for both events (lying on back, feet in stirrups, etc.).

Ellen could not turn on the vacuum cleaner at home because the sound reminded her of the suction machine used during her abortion.

Peggy was forced by her parents to have an abortion when she was eighteen. Afterwards, Peggy's parents bought her a dozen roses "for being so brave." Three years later Peggy has still not been able to look at roses without feeling anxious and sick.

For others it could be the sight of the hosptal or clinic where the abortion was performed, the mention of abortion on radio or television, looking at a child that would be the same age as the aborted baby, and a host of other trigger events that can thrust the parents of aborted children back to a moment in their lives that they deeply regret.[2]

**Anger**. Unresolved bitterness or frustration at those involved in the abortion event. Often it arises from feeling deceived, not being given proper information at the time of the abortion, being compelled to abort, or being treated callously by others. Anger could be directed at:

- *the other parent of the aborted child*. Lois told her husband that she was pregnant. Her husband said to her, "You get rid of that kid or I'm leaving." The following week, Lois aborted her child. Twelve years later her anger at

24

her husband still remains deep within her.

Peter begged his wife not to abort their second child. He told his wife that he would pay her $200 a week to bring the baby to term. Peter's wife aborted in spite of his plea. "I'm lucky I have Joey," Peter said, regarding his first son.

- *those in the clinic*. Jackie recalled how terribly she was treated by the abortionist. While she was lying on the table, the abortionist never spoke a word to her, performed the abortion, rose from the table and said to her, "Now get up," and walked out.

  Other women are angry because they had not been told what would occur during their abortion procedure. This seems especially true of those who have had second- and third-trimester abortions in which they experience labor and give birth to a dead child — many times seeing the child in the arms of the abortion personnel.

- *friends or those who suggested the abortion*. Barbara was told by her friends that the best thing she could do at the time of her pregnancy was to abort. Months later, when Barbara wanted to talk about her regret and sorrow for having aborted, her friends would consistently change the subject.

- *God*. Flo had an abortion performed in Mexico in the early 1950s. She had to drive for hours to get to the clinic. She prayed that God would intervene in some way and stop what she felt compelled to do. "I prayed for 120 miles for him to help me, for him to do something, and he did nothing!" For many years Flo had been unable to express her disappointment that God had not intervened in her time of confusion and need.

**Drug use, alcohol abuse, sexual promiscuity**. In order to escape the emotional pain they have been unable to express; to anesthetize themselves or punish themselves.

Sarah was hospitalized for drug and alcohol abuse. Her addictions could be traced directly back to the period immediately following her abortion.

**Sexual dysfunction**. A loss of interest in sex; using sex as a weapon in relationships; reliving the abortion experience while engaging in sex.

Tory felt angry at her husband while having sex (her husband was the father of the aborted child). Eventually she completely lost interest in sex and was even afraid to engage in it.

Anne would have regular menstrual periods throughout the year until the month of February, when her cycle would be thrown off. It was in that same month that Anne had aborted eight years earlier.

**Phobias and compulsive disorders**. Suddenly being afraid of doctors, being afraid of getting sick or dying, refusing to go past the abortion clinic. Compulsive washing, bulimia or anorexia has been identified in a number of women.

Jane, after her abortion, went home and burned the clothing she wore to the clinic and has a great need to shower a couple of times a day because of a relentless sense of feeling "dirty."

**Inability to express emotions**. A psychic numbing or a loss of the ability to feel or empathize with others. This can occur because the feelings associated with the abortion are too overwhelming, or because the woman or man needs to be able to function in daily life and thus leaves many feelings unresolved and "pushed down."

Laura complained of being unable to care about anything or anyone. She had lost a sensitivity to life and to others after her abortion.

**Fear of other children**. The sight of other children subconsciously reminds the woman or man of the loss of their own child.

Monica could not sit in church and listen to a children's choir singing. Tom had difficulty being in the presence of his nephew and niece after his girlfriend had procured an abortion.

**Inability to attend baptisms or baby showers; finding no joy in another's pregnancy**. These are associated with the feelings of guilt, shame and remorse over a previous abortion.

Dave, the father of an aborted child, was moved with profound grief when he noticed a poster for the film *Three Men and a Baby* while leaving a movie theater. When his friends invited him to see the film, he simply could not attend.

Jenny was a pediatric nurse in a local hospital. Years after her abortion Jenny found herself holding a small infant and crying uncontrollably while saying, "I'm sorry. I'm sorry."

**Inability to relate to the opposite sex**. A distancing from or a lack of confidence and trust in the opposite sex because of deep hurt from a previous abortion experience.

Joan was terrified to date a man for years after her abortion. She found herself increasingly susceptible to homosexual encounters which, she felt, protected her from pregnancy and from being hurt again.

**Fixating on another child**. Psychically connecting with another child to "fill the gap" left by a previous abortion.

Diane fixated on her nephew who had been born around the same time her aborted child would have been born. Diane was buying her nephew "birthday presents" for months after his birth.

**Abuse of other children**. Subsequent children may be the focus of unresolved anger and frustration from a previous abortion — especially if they were expected to be the "perfect child" that the aborted baby was imagined to be, or to fill the emotional gap left by the aborted child. The parent's guilt-induced inability to bond with subsequent children could also cause them to abuse these children physically or emotionally.

Connie gave birth to four children after having aborted her first child. She noticed that her expectations for her oldest child were far greater than for her other children. Connie would be more critical and chastising to her oldest child and realized that she had never truly developed a loving relationship with that girl, who was by then in her mid-teens.

**Atonement baby**. Bringing a child to term that will subconsciously fill the void left by a previously aborted baby. Having a great urge to be pregnant again after an abortion.

Karen aborted twice and was pregnant with her third child which she was bringing to term. She said, "I hope this baby makes up for what I did a couple of years ago."

Debbie aborted fifteen years ago. After the abortion, Debbie's mother became quite ill and needed constant care. The more dependent (or even childlike) Debbie's mother became, the more Debbie would respond enthusiastically in helping her. "My mother became the baby I never had," said Debbie months after her mother died.

**Atonement marriage**. The underlying motivation to be married is to validate an abortion experience, especially if the abortion was procured "for the sake of the relationship."

Tony and Donna were struggling in their marital relationship for years. After months of counseling, both realized that the primary issue in their relational difficulties was the unresolved thoughts and feelings they both had about an abortion which they had procured while they were dating. This couple began to understand how much this event figured in their decision to be married (to cover their feelings of guilt and remorse) and how great an impact it had on the deterioration of their marriage.

**Struggling with what it means to be a parent**. Feeling confused or lacking confidence out of the sense of being unworthy to be a mother or father.

Julie felt terrible when she was with other mothers. She consistently felt unworthy to be part of a mothers' club, P.T.A., etc.

**Anniversary reactions**. A sudden, inexplicable depression or emotional reaction that seems to occur around the same time each year, the time around the date of the abortion, date of conception, or projected date of birth.

Cara, after her abortion, suffered a nervous breakdown on her own birthday. While her family was celebrating the day of her birth, Cara said that she could literally "smell death" and had to be hospitalized.

Mary, in the month of April, found herself crying for no apparent reason until she realized that it was the same month in which she had aborted ten years earlier.

**Survivor guilt**. Found in Vietnam veterans and in Holocaust survivors. The statement, "I survived but my baby didn't," captures the unresolved guilt and shame that many parents of aborted children carry with them.

Helen stated, "I'm not sure I deserve to live after what I did. I can't believe I abandoned my baby."

## Spiritual Impact

Spiritually, many see abortion as their first "serious sin" and the one that is unforgivable by God. Many women and men have stayed away from church or participation in the sacraments because they are convinced that our Lord and the Church could never forgive what they had done. Eileen had an abortion over thirty years ago and had never received Communion since that time. She eventually got married, raised a family of seven, and went to church each week with her husband and children, but, as the rest of her family went up to receive the Eucharist, Eileen would always stay in the pew, never feeling that God could forgive her. Finally, after thirty years she found a priest she could talk with and poured out her soul to him. They celebrated the Sacrament of Penance together, and Eileen received the Eucharist for the first time in all those years on the day her oldest son was married.

Other parents of aborted children fear a vengeful God,

a God that will "settle the score" in some way for what they did. Many interpret subsequent difficulties or hardships as "God getting me back." Many women view a later physical problem or even a hysterectomy as an act of God's vengeful justice. They feel unworthy to pray or to ask for the Lord's help or guidance. Emily was terribly afraid that God would take one of her children because of an abortion she had had years before. She longed to enter her parish church to pray, but never felt worthy enough to do so. All she could do was to carry this deep fear within her, alone, for months.

## Impact on Men

Although women are so often deeply scarred by an abortion experience, men do not leave unscathed by abortion's aftermath either. Many husbands or boyfriends were not part of the decision to abort.

They feel powerless, guilty and angry. The trust which they had thought was part of their relationship was violated. On the other hand, many men were very much part of the decision to abort, often being the person to persuade the woman to destroy her child. Months or years later, these men carry within them a suffocating burden of guilt and sorrow. They feel that at a time when they could have been strong, they were morally weak. They despise themselves for their lack of courage and have a great deal of difficulty expressing their feelings. Deep down, the man's self-understanding as "father" has been compromised. The one who is called to "provide" and "protect" simply did not, and the weight of this reality bears heavily upon the fathers of aborted children. The "strong, silent types" do not fare well after abortion. *Newsweek* addressed this issue in 1988:

> Psychiatrist Dr. Kyle Pruett of Yale University says that many men have no idea of how much they are hurting until afterward. "Then, whammo, they feel very guilty." Counselors recognize a "post-abortion syndrome" that is felt by men as well as women: loss, sorrow,

depression and anger often lasting years after the event.[3]

## Impact on Relationships

The vast majority of evidence indicates that abortions performed for the sake of saving or sustaining a relationship rarely succeed in this aim. If either person is unhappy with the decision to abort, or if either accepts it through moral compromise, resentment and bitterness inevitably follow. Dr. David Reardon, author of *Aborted Women: Silent No More*, has suggested that abortion seems consistently to underscore the weakness in a relationship. As an act of conditional love which reflects an unwillingness to accept an inconvenient child, abortion implies that the love between the couple, too, is conditional. It implies that the relationship will be sustained as long as the partners are convenient to each other.[4] "Choosing to keep the child reaffirms the relationship; choosing to abort calls the relationship into question," says Reardon.[5]

The inability to communicate one's wishes and feelings can both lead to a decision to abort and devastate the life of a relationship afterwards. If one partner remains silent while the couple is discerning what to do about a pregnancy, the other partner will often interpret this silence as acceptance of their decision. When either partner remains silent about his or her ambivalence on a decision to abort, the foundations for hurt and resentment are established which inevitably emerge later in a destructive way.

## Impact on Adolescents

Statistically adolescents (ages 15 to 24) have procured the vast majority of abortions in the past fifteen years. This is of increasing concern to professionals who propose that experiencing the trauma of abortion at such a young age, and being unable emotionally to resolve the death of

31

the child, could stunt emotional growth in adult life. Dr. Wanda Franz has suggested that P.A.S. is most likely to occur as a teenager matures and begins to integrate various facets of personhood (psychic, physical, emotional, spiritual dimensions of life). As Dr. Reardon points out:

> Unfortunately, the problem of post-abortion sequelae among young women is increased by their greater tendency to "bottle up" their emotions after an abortion experience. Thus, even though teens are likely to be the most deeply affected by abortions, they are also likely to be the least expressive about their doubts and pains. Some are emotionally "numbed," others conceal their inner pain. . . . Others strive to conceal their grief, especially from parents who might have encouraged or pressured them to have the abortion, out of fear that expressing any complaint afterwards might further drive a wedge between them and their parents.
>
> It must also be remembered that when a young woman (or man) engages in intercourse, she is seeking much more than physical pleasure. . . . In the broader perspective, intercourse is just a symptom of the young woman's search for love, fulfillment, and maturity. When a young woman is encouraged by her boyfriend, friends, parents, or society to abort rather than to give life to her child, she is being told that her search for love was wrong. . . . Instead of being encouraged to accept the consequences of her choices. . . she is encouraged to "mature" through infantile destruction. Thus she is made to participate in desolation rather than growth; she is exposed to the fear of death rather than the joy of life.[6]

Clearly, the traumatic impact of abortion is wide and deep. The symptoms of Post-Abortion Syndrome and their toll on various dimensions of life are manifesting themselves daily in the lives of countless men and women.

Tragically, the unborn child was not the only one to die on the abortionist's table.

# Notes

1. Sally Tisdale, "We Do Abortions Here" in *Harper's*, October, 1988, p. 70

2. RU486 or the "morning-after pill" should be noted here. At present there is a strong lobby to legitimize the use of this chemical as a "safe means to terminate pregnancy." It should be well understood that RU486 is an abortifacient that can be used up to the eighth to tenth week of pregnancy. From my experience in post-abortion ministry I am particularly alarmed at this fact. For many women and men it was initially very important to maintain physical distance from where the abortion had taken place (for example, by not driving past the abortion clinic) in order to thwart disturbing flashbacks and emotional distress. With RU486 parents will actually be aborting their children in their own places of residence, thus making it impossible to provide the vital safe distance from the event. I shudder to think of the potential horror that RU486 could cause to unborn children and their parents.

3. Tamar Jacoby, "Doesn't a Man Have Any Say?" in *Newsweek*, May 23, 1988, p. 74.

4. David Reardon, *Aborted Women: Silent No More* (Chicago: Loyola Press, 1987), p. 74.

5. ibid., p. 125.

6. ibid., p. 133.

*Chapter Three*

# THERE IS HOPE FOR YOUR FUTURE

---

## The Process of Healing and Reconciliation

God of power and might,
we praise you through your Son, Jesus Christ,
who comes in your name.

He is the Word that brings salvation.
He is the hand you stretch out to sinners.
He is the way that leads to your peace.

*Eucharistic Prayer for Reconciliation II*

### The Effects of Sin and the Hope of Grace

In the Judeo-Christian tradition, the word "sin" and its effects on the human condition have been understood in a variety of ways. The scriptures provide a vast horizon of insight and reflection on this reality. In the Old Testament, sin is described as a breach of an agreement

(Jgs 11:27), disloyalty (1 Sam 19:4), rebellion (Is 1:2), breach of a covenant (Hos 8:1), and folly (Dt 32:6).[1] In short:

> The first and dominant effect of sin is death (cf also Ez 18:4); sin is the denial of life, and one can paraphrase the [Old Testament] by saying that in its view the sinner dies a little each time he sins.[2]

Sin, in our tradition, can be understood, then, as that reality of being human that seeps the life right out of us. Occasions of sinful behavior become foretastes of death, of losing the gift of life graciously bestowed on us. Abortion is "sinful" because it destroys life — the life of a pre-born child. However, it does not stop there. As sin, abortion then begins to suck the interior life out of the child's mother, the child's father, the child's family, and indeed, our very society. The only one who can replace this loss of life is God himself — the giver of all life, visible and invisible.

In the New Testament, the notion of sin is developed even further. Here, sin is understood as lawlessness (1 Jn 3:4), unrighteousness (1 Jn 5:17), a human condition since the fall (Rm 5:12-21); the sinner succumbs to darkness rather than light (Jn 3:19).[3] However, the New Testament writers focus consistently on the victory of grace over sin, life over death, mercy over condemnation, a victory found in the person of Jesus Christ.

> It is remarkable that most of the occurrences of the word [sin] in the Synoptics deal with the forgiveness of sin. Jesus is the conqueror of sin, and it is this which makes Him the associate and friend of sinners whom He calls to repentance (Mt 9:10; Lk 7:34). . . . Jesus. . . did not condone sin; He called to repentance and by His kindness made real to man the divine mercy and disposition to forgive. . . . The sinner need only ask forgiveness (Lk 18:13f). There is joy in heaven at the return of the sinner (Lk 15:7).[4]

It is only the Holy Spirit of Christ, still active in the Church community, that can breathe resurrected life into

35

the dead body of an unborn child. Likewise, only his Spirit can breathe into that child's parents and family a renewed hope, a reconciling embrace. It is this path to hope that our Lord conferred upon his disciples.

> Jesus conferred upon the Twelve the power to forgive sins (Jn 20:21). This can only be understood in light of the personal power exercised by Jesus. This power is communicated through their reception of "a holy spirit," symbolized by the breath of Jesus upon them.[5]

In many ways, the reality of abortion and the healing journey capture both the Old Testament and New Testament understandings of the effects of sin and the ultimate victory of grace.

The task of the healer, whether it be a minister, family member or friend, is to create the context for the parents of an aborted child to encounter the life-giving and reconciling Spirit of God once again — to be a small instrument of our Lord's saving grace and to set an environment for that parent to be reconciled with God, the Church, their unborn child, and finally themselves again.

As a priest, parish minister or friend, we tend to be somewhat at an advantage when we encounter a woman or man who seeks healing after an abortion. Often, by the time a woman comes to us to share her story, she has already identified the source of her pain. "Father, I had an abortion." She has already connected her present distress to an earlier abortion experience. In professional therapy, on the other hand, the post-abortive parent might complain of symptoms associated with post-abortion trauma without making the connection between his/her present distress and an abortion event in the past. For instance, Elaine was seeing a professional counselor for months because of persistent depression. It was only after a significant amount of time went by that Elaine admitted to her counselor that she had had an abortion. Both counselor and patient then understood the close relationship between Elaine's present difficulties and her abortion. After this, Elaine purposely came to a priest to discuss the spiritual impact of her experience.

It is truly wonderful to see how many post-abortive parents seek healing on a spiritual plane. Therefore, the person who comes to a pastoral minister does so because they "know who we are." So often they are searching for a healing of the scars of regret inflicted by memories of the abortion. They seek someone who can lead them to a deep peace and reconciliation whose ultimate source is the Spirit. The parent could have gone to a therapist first. In fact, she might have seen a professional counselor and made great progress in healing, but now she calls upon us as ministers and friends to attend to the spiritual dimension of her life and its ultimate connection to the experience of abortion.

I would like to define the "spiritual" here as the force or dynamism that unites mind, body, emotions, and soul. It is the life-giving dimension of our being that makes us "whole," or "holy." To be in a growing relationship with God, who is the "Holy One," allows us to integrate the various facets of our human personhood. Recall that it is precisely these human dimensions which abortion has broken: the woman's body was violated, her mind cannot look back to her painful past, her emotions are fragmented, and her soul is disengaged from her God. Her life becomes "unglued" and fragmented, and she seeks to find the one who will guide her in putting it back together.

Along with this, I would like to suggest that the post-abortive parent has been plagued by a relentless confusion:

- First, a confusion of *identity:* who am I in light of what happened? Am I still the good, loving person I thought I was?
- Secondly, a confusion of *emotions:* why does it hurt so much? It was supposed to take care of everything. I thought I'd feel relieved after it was over, but I feel terrible.
- Thirdly, a confusion of *meaning:* what is my life all about? What does God think of me? What happened to my baby?

The most precious contribution that a priest or pastoral minister can make for the post-abortive parent basically involves the level of spiritual direction. By creating the umbrella under which each of the facets of a woman's or man's brokenness can be touched and healed the minister truly becomes a vehicle of the grace and peace of Jesus Christ. It is important to remember, though, that by the time a person comes to our door to share their story, they probably have already begun their reconciliation process to some extent. For a person to acknowledge the interior pain left by an abortion is itself a breaking down of denial; and this, in turn, is the stepping stone to healing. The Lord has been touching this person's life and heart with his divine mercy and now s/he wishes to respond to this redemptive grace in a concrete way. The parents of an aborted child seek to understand their healing journey in the context of a faith tradition that will allow them, first, to unite themselves with God, and secondly, to unite themselves with the Church community once again. Through post-abortion ministries like the Catholic Church's Project Rachel, the priest or pastoral minister can represent and symbolize these two realities for the abortive parent in a powerful way. Remember, though, that healing takes time. It is a true journey to wholeness that this person has embarked on. The task of the minister is simply to point the way, to show the path to new life which the Christian tradition has known and sought to follow for ages.

## The Disposition of the Minister

To be true instruments of the Lord's healing grace first demands that we ministers reflect on and understand our own paths to hope which we, ourselves, have taken in life. To recognize the roads which we have traveled through death to resurrection is especially important. What paths has my own journey of suffering taken? In what areas of my life have I been forgiven? healed? reconciled to God, other, myself? In short, what has been my "history of salvation"? We cannot lead another out of the desert unless we have been there ourselves and know the way to freedom. We cannot offer hope if that hope does not arise out of our own struggles and brokenness. We cannot heal the wounds of another unless we are willing to recognize and bind up our own. Empathy for another arises out of the depths of our own brokenness and healing. "You may call God love, you may call God goodness, but the best name for God is compassion," writes the great mystic Meister Eckhart. I think the best name for the minister of healing, too, is "compassion."

A compassionate heart reminds us, as Fr. Michael Mannion has said,[6] that "we have all aborted God's will in some way." In compassion, the post-abortive parent is not a mystery to me, but one who reflects my own capacity to destroy life. Therefore, the encounter between abortion victim and minister demands an act of courage on the victim's part for coming to us and facing such painful memories, and on the minister's part for confronting the wounds within him- or herself. Henri Nouwen explains:

> Through compassion we sense our hope for forgiveness in our friend's eye, and our hatred in their angry speech. When they kill, we know that we could have done it; when they give life, we know that we can do the same.[7]

If I have learned anything during my years as a priest, it is my strengths and weaknesses, what I can and what I cannot do as a minister. This is especially important to know when one is working with an abortion victim. One needs to understand one's limitations in the healing journey. In other words, you might be able to walk with a parent through an abortion experience or possibly through one part of an abortion event, but you might not be able to deal with alcohol or drug abuse, which is also part of the person's life that needs to be healed, or a host of other scars that are beyond your particular capacity to resolve. There could be personalities you cannot deal with because of circumstances in your own life. For example, if you are ministering to a woman who has aborted but who is also dealing with alcoholism and this disease has left unhealed wounds within you, then you might need to refer this person to another competent minister, not only for her sake but for yours. You can be her friend and companion on a particular part of her healing journey, but you are not her savior. The Lord saves us all, and we as ministers of this salvific love must always recognize our gifts and our finitude in sharing this healing grace.

However, if there is one prerequisite to post-abortion ministry, if there is one "must" on the list of requirements, it is a dedicated prayer life. Trying to counsel a person who is filled with regret and grief over a past abortion without prayer is like a doctor's attempting to do heart surgery with a band-aid. In personal prayer I gain the interior space to allow others into my heart and soul and have a greater capacity to absorb the pain and sorrow which they want to share with me. Prayer widens and deepens us. To me, this is the greatest gift the minister can give the post-abortive parent — a sensitive and open heart bound in prayer that has the interior space to hear their story and absorb their sorrow. In this way, the burden of carrying the weight of guilt, shame and grief might be lessened in some way.

## The Environment for Healing

As the personal disposition of the pastoral minister is essential that healing and reconciliation may take place in the mother or father of an aborted child, so too is the environment created by the minister for dialogue. There are three areas of concern that the minister should be especially conscious of when dealing in post-abortion ministry:

- First, it is important that you create a context of *hospitality:* that is, the way you greet the woman or man coming to speak with you. Remember how difficult it must be for anyone to reveal this sin to another person. Therefore, make sure you are calm, focused and ready to greet these parents in a spirit of openness and welcome. If they do not feel "at home" with you, they will often not return.

- Second, you should create a context of *friendship:* that is, the way you relate to the woman or man as they are speaking with you. Be aware of providing an understanding but not condoning atmosphere. Friendship invites another to grow through the "fires" of acceptance and care without the fear of being "burned" by condemnation or ridicule. However, friendship also demands being dedicated to the truth: not covering over the truth of what abortion is but facing the cross, together, with faith and trust in Christ's resurrected life.

- Third, you should create the context of *safety:* that is, the way you respond to what the person is saying. It is extremely important to convey confidentiality. The person needs to know that the environment you have established for them is a place where they can share their thoughts and feelings without fear of others knowing. Do not be surprised if they test you to see how far they can trust your confidence by asking, "Are you going to tell anyone about this?"

We tend to trust only those who we know truly care for our well-being. For the parents of aborted children, too, the hospitality, friendship and safety which we can provide will be the invaluable road which is laid for them to continue their healing journey. Sidney Callahan writes:

In the same way we must use. . . sensitivity and affective attunement to comfort the sorrowful. One must enter into the person's sad state, attune oneself to their unique experience, slow down, be sorrowful as they are sorrowful. When an insensitive person cannot do this and brusquely insists on dismissing pain, or puts it aside too quickly with an instant fix, the suffering person is affronted by the lack of understanding. A com-

41

forter can only begin to help after he or she has been sufficiently attuned to another's experience. Please, don't do something, just stand there — empathetic presence is what is most needed.[8]

A healthy context of affirmation created by the minister will be the foundation on which healing and reconciliation can progress. Drs. Conrad Baars and Anna Terruwe address this issue:

> In relation to mothers and their children we are reminded of another group of human beings direly in need of affirmation; namely, the unborn. The destruction of innocent human life is the most extreme form of non-affirmation. Its effect on the mother is no less grave, since she destroys the very being which is destined to affirm her in its own unique way. . . . Abortion is a form of psychic self-destruction, and if practiced on a large scale it will have the gravest consequences for any society which condones it. Abortion is an act of aggression, not an assertive act. . . . To advise [a woman] to abort is to *deny* her — the very opposite of affirmation — and to push her even deeper into her loneliness and isolation, to provoke a depression which in our experience is malignant and incurable.[8]

In my experience as a spiritual director I have found that affirmation can often generate the interior energy which a person needs in order to walk the path of reconciliation and healing. It is essential that post-abortion victims see themselves in a positive light. Therefore, do not hesitate to affirm their goodness. Tell them that you think it is great that they came to you seeking help. Tell them how honored you are that they have invited you into their lives and have the courage to share their pain and sorrow with you. Tell them that you really believe that God brought them to this point, that it was his Spirit guiding them to find healing and peace. Affirmation breeds confidence, and confidence (i.e., faith in oneself) generates the interior energy needed to continue the journey back to life.

Creating the affirming context of hospitality, friendship and safety allows a person to break down the interior walls of defense which they have built in order to protect themselves from their own feelings. As mentioned in Chapter One, defense mechanisms (denial, rationalization, repression, avoidance etc.) help us feel safe. When our external environment is not a safe place in which to share our true thoughts and feelings, then we build up interior safety mechanisms (i.e., defenses) to help us feel secure. If a person feels secure in their external environment, then they will be able to break down the interior walls of defense which they have been employing. However, the minister cannot try to break down these interior defenses himself. If he tries, they will simply build them up again. All the minister is called to do is to create the context whereby the persons will feel safe enough to lower their defenses and reveal their deepest feelings.

Dr. Ian Kent had observed fifty women who gave a variety of reasons for entering psychotherapy, none related to abortion. After a long period of therapy, when they had developed a deep trust relationship with the therapist, they revealed a previous abortion and began to express feelings of mourning, love, regret and identification with their aborted child. Dr. Kent wondered about the discrepancy between his own observations and the many studies claiming little or no negative effects of abortion. He and his colleagues designed a typical questionnaire and did a study of seventy-two women — and got the same results as other studies: little or no effects. . . . But, in examining the data more closely, he concluded that the very absence of effect was really emotional numbness, a significant negative effect in itself. Dr. Kent believes that the hurt of abortion is so deep that it is repressed and will rarely be revealed outside of a deep trust relationship.[10]

It is this "deep trust relationship" which the minister of healing can foster through the affirming gifts of hospitality, friendship and safety for the post-abortive parent.

## Instruments of Grace

Throughout its history, the Catholic community has consistently encountered the grace of Christ through three primary avenues of faith: scriptures, sacraments and the Church. It is precisely these dimensions of the community's faith life which can be the most valuable instruments of reconciliation and wholeness for the mother or father of an aborted child.

Reflecting on and praying about the history of salvation as it is revealed through the word of God can be a very important mode of healing for the aborted child's parents. Through the scriptures, the father or mother can understand their own history of salvation. They can encounter a healing and forgiving Lord, a Lord that takes the initiative to forgive, a God that wants them to return to him, a savior who dies for them. Also, using the scriptures helps a parent to realize that people through the ages were subject to sin and grievous mistakes but were also forgiven by God. Post-abortive parents can find many of their own thoughts and emotions expressed in passages in scriptural books like the Psalms, and these become a source of strength, insight and comfort. The minister might find that Ignatian techniques of prayer and reflection could be useful here: i.e., allowing the woman or man to visualize specific scenes in the scriptures and to place themselves in these biblical moments of encountering the Lord. Finally, the scriptures can be a powerful mode of healing if the man or woman is invited to reflect on various figures in the Bible whose experiences, in some way, parallel their own: Mary Magdalen, Peter, Paul, Rachel, or Mary, the mother of Jesus, to name a few whose lives and relationship with God have helped parents of aborted children understand their own story a bit more.

In short, praying with the aborted parent during each counseling session is not only valuable but essential. Prayer of any kind invites the mother or father to understand the cross of abortion which they bear, within the wider context of faith and hope in God's mercy and for-

44

giveness. I recommend that prayer both begin and end each session. If the parent is unable to pray at a particular time, the minister should then pray on behalf of the parent, drawing into the prayer what was shared in that particular session. The minister, here, needs to be sensitive to the parent's established relationship with God and the style of prayer that he or she employs.

> During a counseling session some pastoral counselors pray with the person they are counseling. Praying with a person has a twofold benefit: it calls upon God's help for the enterprise and it serves as a model of prayer for the counselee. The counselor who is a person of faith and aware of God's presence in his or her life is quite likely to inspire a similar awareness in the counselee. If the counselor manifests an open trust in God's providence, the counselee is apt to be influenced by this trust and develop a similar trust. To be effective as a pastoral counselor you need to be a person of faith; it is not enough to be just well trained in psychological skills and techniques.[11]

In the Catholic Church the celebration of the sacraments has always been the prime means for the community to encounter the Lord's transforming grace. Therefore the sacraments are an essential part of the healing process for the Catholic parent of an aborted child. The sacrament of Penance is not an isolated event outside the healing process. Rather, it is integral to celebrating the man or woman's entire journey of healing and forgiveness. It is a special engraced moment that can sum up the journey of healing and rejoicing in Christ's saving and reconciling love, both in the past and into the mystery of the future.

When is the celebration of the sacrament appropriate? When the aborted parent's image of God is a positive one. Therefore, it is important for the priest or minister to know how the woman or man understands their relationship with God before inviting them to the celebration of the sacrament. If they see God as the "scolding father" or the one who could never forgive what they had done, then they are probably not ready to celebrate the sacra-

45

ment in a full way. Also, the priest or minister must gauge whether or not the parent is ready to accept forgiveness. It is essential, as well, to ensure that there is a positive attitude toward self if the celebration of the sacrament is going to be most fruitful. Asking questions like "What does God think of you? What would he say to you?" can help in getting a clearer picture as to where a particular person is in their relationship with the Lord and in their healing process.

For some, the desire to be reconciled with God and the Church through the sacrament comes up immediately. For these parents, their hurt is so suffocating that they do not have the interior energy to take part in the process of healing until they have been "re-energized" by the celebration of the sacrament. If this is the case, then the priest should celebrate the sacrament but make clear to the woman or man that the sacrament should be understood as a point of departure to continue the healing journey. It is important, also, to be aware of the "spiritual high" that can come from celebrating the sacrament in the early stages of the process which leaves a person susceptible to falling back into denial once the initial feelings of peace and well-being have worn off. The priest should encourage the person to continue the process of healing and to confront their difficult recollections and emotions in the same spirit of faith and trust in God in which they initially celebrated the sacrament.

While celebrating the sacrament of Penance, especially if you are encountering a particular post-abortive parent for the first time, may I suggest to the priest to observe the following "acknowledgements" that might prove helpful in the celebration:

- Acknowledge their courage for coming to the sacrament and sharing the abortion event with you.

- In a spirit of gentleness but truth, acknowledge the sin of abortion and what sin does to all of us.

- Acknowledge their pain and sorrow which is evident to you in their seeking forgiveness.

46

- Acknowledge the fact that scars take time to heal, and invite them to contact you so that their healing journey may continue.

- Offer an appropriate penance and absolution.[12]

The confessor should take into account the ecclesiastical nature of abortion as a sin and its ramifications with regard to the laws of the Church. Excommunication and its association with abortion can be confusing to many people. While abortion, according to the 1983 Code of Canon Law, incurs an automatic penalty of excommunication, it is important for the confessor to discern whether the automatic penalty applies to a particular person. It will depend upon the circumstances in which the abortion was procured. For excommunication to be operative, two things are required at the time of the act in question. *First*, the person must have full knowledge, (1) that abortion is not only a serious sin but also a crime in Canon Law; (2) that this crime carries the penalty of excommunication. *Second*, the person must have acted freely and with malice; no internal or external force must have been brought to bear in the decision to abort and in the carrying out of the act.

The law proposes that the following people do not incur excommunication for procuring a successful abortion:

1. a person with only the imperfect use of reason
2. a person who lacked the use of reason due to drunkenness or other culpable mental disturbance
3. a person so overwhelmed by the situation that they were not able to think clearly at the time
4. a minor who had not celebrated their 18th birthday
5. a person who was forced through grave fear, even if only relatively grave; or through necessity or serious inconvenience. Thus someone who is forced through fear does not incur the penalty, even with an intrinsically evil act like abortion.
6. a person who had been gravely and unjustly provoked into the action

7. a person who, without fault, was unaware that abortion incurred such a penalty.

In short, abortion is punishable by excommunication when all the requirements for this sanction have been fulfilled and none of the above-mentioned nullifying factors exists. From my pastoral experience of working with parents of aborted children, proving that a person has actually incurred excommunication can be very difficult. In order to do this the priest/confessor must consider the age of the person at the time of the abortion; the person's emotional and psychological condition; the degree of knowledge the person had about the Church's law and about penalties attached to the law; the degree of willfulness and freedom present; outside circumstances, legal principles, principles of interpretation, etc.

If excommunication has been incurred, it must be lifted in order for the person to enter fully into the Church's life once again. By law, the lifting of an automatic penalty, such as that incurred by abortion, is reserved to the local Ordinary (the bishop of a diocese). This power is part of the ordinary power a bishop has in virtue of his office. However, the Church allows the bishop to delegate his ordinary power to the priests of his diocese. In many if not most dioceses around the country, priests have received the faculty to lift the sanction of excommunication during the celebration of the sacrament of Penance.[13]

The sacrament of Anointing can be a powerful moment in one's healing journey.[14] Whether one is dealing with emotional or physical pain, the celebration of the Lord's saving grace in this sacrament can bring a deep sense of peace, consolation and hope to those who are suffering. Therefore, this rite can be an appropriate setting in which the post-abortive parent can encounter God's presence and love in a specific way. However, the priest should understand that the sacrament can only be conferred when a person's mental or physical health is seriously impaired: for instance, in the case of deep, chronic depression, suicidal thoughts or attempts, or uterine scarring.

Finally, once the person has confessed their sin and acknowledged their need for forgiveness in the sacrament of Penance, the celebration and reception of the Eucharist can truly be their "divine food for the journey" to sustain and strengthen them as they continue along the path to wholeness. So many women and men have testified how important the Eucharist was to their ability and willingness to confront the darkness of their sin. Knowing that Christ was with them through the sacrament gave them the confidence in God and in themselves to face their abortion experience squarely.

However, it should be noted here that reception of the Eucharist should not become a way of denying that more healing is needed in a particular person's journey. There may be cases in which the priest or minister would need to discuss truthfully with the parent whether abstaining from the Eucharist might, for a certain period, aid in confronting issues that have not yet been faced. Abstinence here becomes not a vehicle to punish, but rather a way to invite a person to encounter the areas of their lives that need to be addressed and healed. In the majority of cases, however, the Eucharist, along with counseling, will be a powerful means of sustenance and comfort for those on their journey to wholeness.

In the same way, prayer is absolutely essential for the woman and man to come to true peace and reconciliation. The minister should make a conscious effort to pray with the parent each time they meet, and to encourage the person to pray each day in the way they find most comfortable. Prayer, though, should not be used as "divine valium" — that is, as another way to deny or escape painful feelings or recollections. Rather, prayer in any form should be an invitation to speak and to listen to the Lord in a spirit of trust and honesty: an opportunity for a woman or man to express such feelings as anger, regret or sorrow in faith and hope.

Prayer and the celebration of the sacraments implicitly have a communal dimension. The search for wholeness in the post-abortive parent reminds all of us, the entire Church community, that we too are on that same path, both as individuals and as a community of faith. We are a Church of sinners, a "pilgrim people" continually striving to embody the grace of Christ which we have received. Thus it is the community that becomes the instrument of reconciliation for the sinner. At each celebration of the sacraments, the Church prays with and for others in a spirit of unity and peace. The parents of an aborted child need to know that they are accepted back into the community of the faithful. They are still our brothers and sisters in the Lord and we welcome them back to continue their journey with us as one body of faith. The sacraments, then, become a reunion not only with God but with the Church.

## A Basic Methodology for Reconciliation and Healing

What should happen when a man or woman comes to us as pastoral ministers and shares his or her regret and grief over an abortion? How can we respond? How can we contribute to their healing? I would like to propose a basic methodology for ministers that has been used by many who are involved with Project Rachel ministries throughout the country, as an effective means of working with a post-abortive parent. Remember, you are encountering someone who has most likely spent a significant period of time unable to grieve openly over the loss of a child. They have had to employ a host of defense mechanisms to deal with their unresolved feelings of sadness and loss. Also, they are trying to reconcile the guilt and regret they feel for making the decision to destroy their child. Their baby did not simply *die* in the passive sense (for example, through illness or accident). Their child *was killed*, and it is this terrible reality which parents need to embrace, and to which they must be reconciled.

For decades the "classic stages of grief" established by Elizabeth Kubler Ross have been used to understand patterns of grief which all of us go through when we lose someone significant in our lives. Many counselors are observing the same dimensions of the grieving process in the post-abortive parent. The task of the pastoral minister, then, is to aid the parent through these stages of grief and healing. The aim here is not to force a person through the stages of grief, but simply to be an instrument that can aid someone through the process. It is essential for the minister to be aware, however, that these stages of grief are not necessarily "static," but "fluid." In other words, one need not assume that a woman or man begins with the stage of denial and in a certain amount of time will reach the stage of acceptance. A person can easily fluctuate between various stages depending upon where they are in their healing journey. Therefore the minister needs to be sensitive to what the person is saying, in order to discern what dimensions of the grieving process they are trying to express and work through.

As we mentioned earlier, denial is a defense mechanism which protects the woman or man from the emotional and spiritual impact of abortion. At a primary stage of grief, persons in denial seek to keep themselves safe from difficult memories and feelings. The more a person is able to reflect back on a particular event in their life, the more likely denial will be lessened and the painful emotions can begin to be resolved. When a person initially comes to speak about an abortion, levels of denial can still be operative even though the event is acknowledged. I would like to suggest to the minister that, at this initial point in your relationship with a post-abortive parent, you simply allow them to tell you their story, to say as much or as little as they wish. By doing so, the person will get a sense of how far they can entrust their story to you. They will be "feeling you out" to determine how far they can let their guard down. Your task here as minister is to listen sensitively and compassionately. As the person becomes more comfortable with you, they will be able to face the abortion more squarely.

It is extremely important to convey confidentiality at this point. The post-abortive parent needs to know that they can share their story with no risk of others being told. The minister might suggest reviewing some of the symptoms of P.A.S. to help the parent reflect on exactly how their experience of abortion has influenced their lives. This can also be an apt point of departure for subsequent dialogue.

The minister should invite the mother or father of an aborted child to place the abortion experience in a time frame, a chronology. Here the dialogue can center on as many objective details as can possibly be remembered: what happened before, during and after the abortion. For instance:

*Before.* When did she discover she was pregnant? Whom did she tell first? How did he find out about the pregnancy? What was his initial reaction? When did they decide to abort? Who made the decision?

*During.* Where did the abortion take place? What time was it performed? What did the facility look like? How did she get to the clinic? Where did she go after the abortion was over?

*After.* What happened after the abortion? What occurred the following day? How did she feel physically after the abortion?

In other words, the minister should ask as many objective questions as he or she can think of. Why? Because this helps break denial. The abortion becomes very real once again, and the person is given the opportunity to deal with a reality which they were trying for years to forget. As one can imagine, this can be a painful process for the father or mother of an aborted child. The minister needs to be extremely sensitive, supportive and patient here. In general, one will get a good idea of the depth of the person's denial by noting how willing or able they are to recall the facts surrounding the event itself.

If the minister listens carefully, he or she can usually hear the parent express feelings as they recall what occurred in the events connected with their abortion. For instance, Jennifer told me, "As I was sitting in the waiting room I saw so many women [fact] and my heart sank [feeling]." The task of the healer at this point is to guide the parent in getting in touch with the feelings she experienced in connection with their abortion. For example:

How did she feel when she found out she was pregnant?
How did she feel when the decision to abort was firmly made?
How did she feel the day before, the day of the abortion, the day after?
How did she feel in the waiting room? on the table?
How did she feel when what really occurred at the abortion started to make its impact?

This can be a very difficult but cleansing time for the person, as well as a time of insight. Lucy, reflecting on her feelings surrounding her abortion seven years earlier, suddenly said, "You know, Father, I really wanted to keep that baby! It just occurred to me. Deep down, I wanted that baby." Painful feelings often rise to the surface during this time and the post-abortive parent begins to grieve deeply. No matter how difficult these feelings may be, the minister should not be inclined to rescue the parents from them. Rather, let them feel what they have been unable to feel for years. Your gift is your presence, your willingness to be there with them as they work through the grieving process. As feelings and emotions are reflected upon and affirmed, it is at this point that one is likely to see the next three stages of grief expressed.

As the parent is able to express their feelings, they are freer to acknowledge their child's humanity. This admission can be very painful, and the minister will often witness deep emotions being expressed at this time. The stage of **anger** usually arises at this time, when the parent begins to understand how the outcome of the abortion — the death of their child — was, in its drastic finality, all out of proportion to the reasons for which the abortion was procured. Anger can be focused in various directions: at others involved with the event, at God, at oneself. The minister should help in identifying where the anger is directed and understanding it in light of the abortion. Beginning to work on forgiveness is also quite appropriate at this stage. However, remember not to rescue the person from their anger, but guide them in working through it in a spirit of faith. At whom are they angry? Why are they angry? How can their anger be relieved?

When a post-abortive parent experiences emotions that have been repressed, sometimes for years, they are susceptible to trying to relieve their feelings of regret, sorrow and loss through the next stage of grief, called **bargaining**. Here a parent attempts to compensate by their present actions for what they did in the past: for example, having another child in order to "atone" for the aborted child; wanting to be the "perfect parent" in order to bargain away feelings of guilt and mourning; wanting to join Birthright or another volunteer organization as a way of masking their feelings of grief and regret. The minister should help the parent to recognize their bargaining and to understand it in relation to their unresolved emotions. However, it is also important for the minister gently to help the parent to realize that there is nothing they can do to make up for what happened. The baby is gone and nothing will bring the child back.

When the parents of an aborted child acknowledge, sometimes only in the depths of their hearts, that the child has died and there is nothing they can do to reverse this, a deep sadness ensues. A true sense of loss and emptiness can be experienced. The stage of **depression** can be noticed at this point. Here the parent understands the abortion event as a profound deprivation: it has deprived them of knowing their son or daughter. Helping a person to talk can help in relieving depression. The minister's task is to encourage the parent to keep working through their painful feelings. So many parents of aborted children think they have no right to be sad. The minister can acknowledge the parents' sadness at the loss of their child and affirm their right to these feelings. Every mother or father who loses a child is deeply hurt and has a right to feel this loss. The minister can provide the environment for these feelings to be affirmed and worked through.

The stage of depression often passes when the parent is ready and able to *re*personalize their child. For years the child has had to remain *de*personalized and distant. Now comes the final stage of healing called **acceptance**. Here the child is no longer an impersonal being but "my son," "my daughter," whom I acknowledge and embrace. The parent accepts the child, acknowledges the child's death and their responsibility for it, and petitions the Lord to bring the child into his everlasting life. The doctrine of the Communion of Saints can be a hope-filled source of peace for many parents of aborted children. They find great solace in knowing that their child lives on in God's eternal life and now prays for the parents' healing. At this point the minister can invite the parents to name their child. Why? Because then the child is truly theirs. Naming the child, too, can be a powerful means of reconciliation. The parents can also be invited to visualize what the child would have looked like. I am continually amazed at how many parents have already done so in the depth of their hearts.

In my own ministry I have found that writing can be an extremely important exercise in the healing and reconciliation process. It helps the post-abortive parent to "enflesh" their thoughts and feelings. Letter writing in particular has been beneficial to numbers of parents. Writing a letter to God, to the child, to those involved with the abortion decision can help in the process of forgiveness. Many parents find that the most difficult part of their journey of forgiveness is their inability to forgive themselves. Often they wish to dissociate themselves from the person they were when they decided to abort. This frequently leaves them in a state of denial and prevents completion of the healing process. At this stage many parents have been helped by writing a letter to themselves and thereby entering into dialogue with the person they were at the time of the abortion. Through this exercise many have been able to acknowledge feelings of self-contempt and deep sorrow for what they did, and also to reconcile themselves to their painful past.

Journaling, or keeping daily reflections in a personal log, can also be of great assistance to these parents. The person is able to understand and attend to patterns and themes that recur during the journaling. The minister, as well, is likely to see more clearly the progress of healing being made and the areas that continue to be unresolved within the parent.

The minister can gauge the level of healing experienced by a particular person by asking such questions as: What does God think of you? What would he say to you? What does your child think of you? What would he or she say to you? How do you feel about yourself? A response of contempt or an inability to be reconciled indicates that more work between minister and parent is needed. The focus here is on the continual need to make peace with God, oneself and others.

Symbols of the Catholic baptismal liturgy are available to the pastoral minister as vehicles of healing and hope for the post-abortive parent. Presenting the parent with the white baptismal garment and baptismal candle in a paraliturgical setting can bring powerful moments of peace and faith to many mothers and fathers of aborted children. Celebrating a Mass in memory of an aborted child is also afforded those in the Catholic community. This can be especially poignant on specific dates connected with the abortion: the date of the abortion itself, the projected date of birth, or even the feast day of the saint for whom the child was named. Many women and men have found bearing a personal symbol of their child to be an important vehicle for healing and peace: a small Hummel-like figurine to place in their home, a cross to wear around their neck in remembrance, a ring or a plaque to hang, placing flowers at a cemetery — any symbol that will be very personal and a source of both memory and hope. The task of the minister here is to help the parent ritualize their grief in whatever ways are appropriate and helpful.

If the minister is adept at certain advanced techniques of healing, such as Dream Analysis, these can be very helpful. Dreams are often ways for the mind to heal itself, the mind presenting to itself material that it can handle in a safe way. Many repressed thoughts and feelings are expressed through our dream life. It is not surprising that many post-abortive parents have shared specific recurring dreams that, upon good analysis, were shown to have a direct connection to unresolved material from a previous abortion. Rebecca had an abortion eight years ago. Recently she had a recurring dream about encountering an eight-year-old boy sitting on a rock in a field. When Rebecca saw the boy in her dreams, she noticed that he had no facial characteristics, nor would he respond when she called out to him. I asked Rebecca whether she had ever named her unborn child or thought of what her child might have looked like. It was then that Rebecca understood the undeveloped parts of her dream sequence that longed for completion.

Guided imagery has also been used as a means of healing. Here the minister can invite the parent of the aborted child to visualize various moments of the abortion event while also seeing the presence of Jesus by their side as they experience their "cross." The healing of memories can be greatly enhanced through this type of faith visualization.

Creating an environment in which the parents of aborted children can gather to pray and reflect on their experience has been an invaluable instrument of healing and hope for many. Group process allows these mothers and fathers to share their feelings and insights with one another. By doing so they can gain strength, support and encouragement to continue their individual healing journeys. Much like the Alcoholics Anonymous process (including the themes articulated in the "twelve steps"), support groups for the parents of aborted children demand honesty, humility, affirmation and trust. Once this context is established within a group, rapid progress is often made. Programs such as *Women in Ramah: A Post-Abortion Bible Study*[15] have been effective models for structuring a support group. Most importantly, though, this type of experience provides special moments of community that show these parents that they are not alone. There are others "out there" who are on the same healing journey. Deep and enduring friendships often result when one opens one's heart and is understood and accepted by others. For the parents of aborted children the bonds of friendship forged in a group context can well be life-sustaining.

The process of healing, then, is brought to fruition as the relationship between parent and child changes from "I-It" to "I-Thou," from denial to affirmation, from despair to hope. Is there any closure to this process? Yes and no. There will always be memories and a certain degree of sadness for the parents of an aborted child. Any mother or father who loses a son or daughter carries the pangs of heartbreak within them, no matter how far they have come in their healing journey. This is understandable and appropriate. However, strictly speaking there should be some type of closure to the healing process. The relationship between minister and post-abortive parent should come to some discernible end when both feel that healing has progressed to a point where the woman or man can proceed with a life of faith and hope for the future. It is quite appropriate for the minister to invite the parent to some concrete action as a way of thanking the Lord for the healing he has given them. Perhaps this could mean doing some charitable work, donating money to a life-giving cause, or speaking publicly about their journey from death to life.

The minister should understand the nature and limitations of his or her own capacity and competence for journeying with another through the healing process. There could well come a time when a professional therapist needs to be called upon to aid the parent in this process. Therefore a good and competent list of referrals is essential. Since abortion is understood in light of a clinical reality (Post-Traumatic Stress), it might be beneficial for the minister to suggest ongoing professional therapy to the post-abortive parent so that the parent can continue to grow in knowledge of themselves and others. However, be sure that those professionals to whom you refer a parent are deeply sensitive to the spiritual life and to abortion as a traumatic event. It is of great benefit for counselor and minister to work together in providing a context of health and healing for the mother or father of an aborted child.

Finally, as mentioned previously, the celebration of the sacrament of Penance is an integral dimension to the journey of healing and wholeness for those in the Catholic community. It is here that the post-abortive parent can experience the forgiving grace of the Lord in a unique and life-giving way. The celebration of the sacrament truly sums up and celebrates the entire healing journey which the person has been on. It is most appropriately celebrated when the parent has a positive image of God and is ready to accept forgiveness and reconciliation. Our task as ministers of the Gospel is to help these hurting mothers and fathers find meaning in the tragedy which has so profoundly affected their lives. In doing so, we can be paths to hope.

Our Christian faith is surprisingly simple when it faces the reality of sin and death. In the passion and death of our Lord we understand that suffering, death and meaninglessness do not have the last word. Ultimately they will lose out. They will lose out to life; they will lose out to God's redeeming love. In the same way, those who carry the cross of abortion on their shoulders, who bear its suffering, death and meaninglessness within their own hearts, can be given a word of resurrected life and hope. Abortion was not the last word for the unborn child, nor for that child's parents. Just as the disciples look back at Calvary through the prism of the resurrection, so too do the parents of an aborted child look back at their own Calvary through the prism of resurrected faith and hope in God's life-giving and reconciling love.

May the words of the loving Father of the prodigal son find a home in us so that we might look upon those who bear the pain of abortion, who seek to be reconciled and made whole, and share the message of joy only to be found in Life, only to be found in God:

> Let us rejoice and celebrate.
> For these sisters and brothers of ours
>     were dead and have come back to life.
> They were lost, and are found.

# Notes

1. John L. McKenzie, S.J., *Dictionary of the Bible* (New York: Macmillan Publishing Co., Inc., 1965), p. 819.
2. ibid., p. 820.
3. ibid., p. 820.
4. ibid., p. 820.
5. ibid., p. 285.
6. Presentation at the Healing Vision Conference, 1989.
7. Henri Nouwen, *The Wounded Healer* (New York: Doubleday Inc., 1972), p. 41.
8. Sidney Callahan, *With All Our Heart and Mind* (New York: Crossroad, 1988), p. 113.
9. Conrad Baars, M.D., and Anna Terruwe, M.D., *Healing the Unaffirmed: Recognizing Deprivation Neurosis* (New York: Alba House, 1976), pp. 195-7.
10. Matthew and Dennis Linn, and Sheila Fabricant, *At Peace with the Unborn* (New York: Paulist Press, 1985), pp. 20f.
11. Richard P. Vaughan, S.J., *Basic Skills for Christian Counselors* (New York: Paulist Press, 1987), pp. 39f.
12. As to what constitutes an "appropriate penance," I leave this to the pastoral sensitivity and expertise of the confessor. However, I would suggest that the penance include both prayer and some concrete action. The latter might include giving money to a life-giving cause, volunteering one's time for a particular group, etc. It is very important that such a penitential activity have a definite purpose and end. Otherwise there is the danger that the parent will form the impression that the penitential practice is a way to "make up" for the abortion, and thus will use it as a bargaining tool with God (and ultimately themselves). If this occurs, the parent may neglect the deeper dimensions of his or her life that need healing and reconciliation. The confessor must make clear that the penitential exercise is simply one part of the journey to wholeness, that forgiveness is a process, and that it would be well for priest and parent to continue their dialogue outside of the celebration of the sacrament at a later time.
13. *The Code of Canon Law*. Michigan: William Eerdman Publishing Co., 1983. See especially Canons 1398, 1355, 1324, 1323, 1325, 137.

14. The commentary for the Code of Canon Law states: "Those who are judged to have a serious mental illness and who would be strengthened by the sacrament may be anointed" (*Pastoral Care*, 27 [n. 53] ). Considering that Post-Abortion Syndrome is understood under the clinical heading of Post-Traumatic Stress, it would seem legitimate for the minister to celebrate the Sacrament of Anointing if, using pastoral discretion, he deems it helpful in the process of healing.

The emotional and spiritual healing that Anointing can bring is directly alluded to in the liturgical texts themselves. For instance, the prayer of "Blessings of Oil" in the Sacrament of Anointing (cf. *The Rites*, New York: Pueblo, p. 602, #75) states: "May your blessing come upon all who are anointed with this oil, that they may be freed from pain and illness and made well again in body, mind and soul."

15. *Women in Ramah: a Post-Abortion Bible Study*. Christian Action Council, 701 West Broad Street, Suite 405, Falls Church, VA 22046

# REFLECTIONS

Dear God,

I've reached a point in my life now where I need you more than ever before. Because now, Lord, I've lost my little girl; and on top of the terrible grief that under normal circumstances a parent would grieve for a child, I have to live with the truth that it was I who took my child's life.

I know you love me because you even loved those who took the life of your own son, Jesus. And I need to believe in your forgiveness and in my child's forgiveness before I can ever come to forgive myself.

Help me to feel that forgiveness, Lord, so that I may become a whole person again. I'm ripped apart, hating a part of myself that I can never get rid of. I have to bring that part of me back if I'm ever to feel whole again.

I've unjustly accused you of deserting me, when it was I who shut you out. I'm sorry, Lord. Let me never shut you out again. No matter what trials you send my way, let me feel your love and see them through. Help me to deal with my guilt that I may stop making excuses to avoid the pain. I know that you've entrusted me to Fr. John for now. I trust him and feel your presence when I am with him. Help him to help me and all the others who share the pain of the sin we have committed. Keep us all in your care and help us heal. And, most of all, Lord, take care of our children. We have placed them in your loving arms. Let Mary, the mother of us all, care for them until we are reunited with them. Assure our children of how much we love and miss them.

Thank you, Lord,
Cathy

Dear Annie,

I don't know how to begin. If you were here, I know that I'd hold you so tight and I wouldn't ever let you go. And I'd cry and you'd cry and we wouldn't need words, would we? But you're not here, and it's my fault. I wish I could go back in time and change things, but I can't, and I can't bring you back.

I was scared, Annie, real scared. You must have sensed it because they say that a baby in the womb does sense its mother's emotions. You were so very young, helpless and tiny. I let you down, and I'm so sorry. I was afraid I wasn't ready for you. I knew your father, but I didn't know you. I was afraid I'd hurt him and spoil all our chances of a nice, safe, secure life. I was confused and very weak. My heart told me how much I wanted you, and that it would all be OK, but I didn't listen to it.

I wanted you, Annie. I really always wanted you. I want you to believe that. I'm just sorry I didn't follow my heart instead of my head. We can't be together in this life because of what I did, but we will be together one day in a better one. Will you wait for me? Will you forgive me and pray for me?

What I'm going through now, Annie, is very painful. But I find some comfort in knowing that you are safe with God. There are very special people there with you — three of your grandparents. Ask them to pray for me, Annie, and for your father, too. Help us to forgive each other and ourselves. Help us to have faith.

Forgive me. Forgive my fear and my ignorance. Forgive my lack of faith and trust in God. When I go to visit grandma's grave from now on, I'm going to put flowers there for you, too. I always put lilac for grandma. I have a feeling you would like pink. When you see them, let them remind you of my love, and let our tears mix with the rain to keep them alive year after year, as a symbol of our love. Goodbye, for now, my daughter. Until we meet again,

Mommy

Dear Katie,

Look, we've been through an awful lot together, haven't we? And I'm sure we'll be through a lot more in the future. So we've got to get "whole" again. You were always trying to make people happy. All your life you only wanted people to love you, to do what you thought they wanted you to do. If you made them happy, then you would be happy, and everything would work out fine. To accomplish this, you often put aside your needs, your wants, your desires. You swallowed your pride and loosened your morals. You lied to others and to yourself. But just once, kid, you went too far. You took a life to end your pain and confusion and Billy's pain. You figured you would make Billy happy again so you'd both be happy like you were before. But it didn't work this time. You were weak and had lost a sense of yourself. Since then, the pain has been brewing inside of you relentlessly. It's time we deal with it.

I know you really wanted the baby, but you cared too much about what others thought. Well, you're paying for it now, and you will the rest of your life. Because you'll never feel that baby in your arms, or look in her eyes and see the specialness she was to be created for. Forever, you'll wonder what she would have looked like, what she might have become. She might have made a very important contribution to the world. Who knows? But she's gone now. You never gave her a chance.

I don't know if I can ever forgive you, but I am going to try with the help of God, my unborn child, and Fr. John.

Katie

What foolish mortals we all are
to allow the world to dictate to us
what our hearts know to be wrong.

How weak and lost and alone we feel,
even while they are all talking at once.
It was so hard to separate the voices.

The truth isn't always the loudest.

The deed was done;
but now the pain.
So strong after all these years.
Stepped on, pushed aside,
anything to prevent the truth.

But now it's known.
Are you at peace? It's my only comfort.
Denied the chance to live, you were;
But not, my child, to love.

My journey is longer,
but I will find the Light.
For now, seek comfort in God's arms,
till my own can embrace you.

*Written by*
*The mother of an aborted child*
*1988*

## *Appendix Two*

# Prayers of Mercy
# and Commendation

God of all consolation and mercy,
searcher of mind and heart,
the faith of this parent [N.] is known to you alone.

Comfort him/her with the knowledge
that the child for whom he/she grieves
is now entrusted to your loving care.

Through your mercy and forgiveness
bestow upon [N.] the gift of your reconciling love.

We ask this through our Lord Jesus Christ, your Son,
who lives and reigns with you and the Holy Spirit,
one God, forever and ever.

**R. Amen.**

You are the author and sustainer of our lives,
    O God,
you are our final home.
We commend to you [N.] this child.

Trusting in your mercy
and in your all embracing love,
we pray that you give him/her happiness forever.

Turn also to [N.] who has suffered this loss
    through sin.
Confirm him/her in faith, in hope, and in
    reconciling love.
Help [N.] to bear your mercy and peace

so that he/she may one day stand together with
    his/her child
in praising you forever.

We ask this in the name of your Son,
Jesus Christ, our Lord.

**R. Amen.**

Lord God,
ever caring and gentle,
we commit to your love this little one [N.]
Enfold him/her in eternal life.

We pray for his/her parent [N.]
who is saddened and remorseful at the loss of
    his/her child.
Give him/her strength and courage
and help [N.] in his/her pain and sorrow.
May parent and child both meet one day in the
    peace of your kingdom.

We ask this through Christ our Lord.

**R. Amen.**

The official liturgical text of the Order for the Blessing of Parents after a Miscarriage, chapter 1, IX of the *Book of Blessings* is given below. The prayers contained in this rite may be suitably adapted for use with parents after an abortion. In particular circumstances, it may be appropriate that the celebration of the sacrament of Penance precede the use of this rite.

# ORDER FOR THE BLESSING OF PARENTS AFTER A MISCARRIAGE

## INTRODUCTION

279    In times of death and grief the Christian turns to the Lord for consolation and strength. This is especially true when a child dies before birth. This blessing is provided to assist the parents in their grief and console them with the blessing of God.

280    The minister should be attentive to the needs of the parents and other family members and to this end the introduction to the *Order of Christian Funerals*, Part II: Funeral Rites For Children will be helpful.

281    These orders may be used by a priest or a deacon, and also by a layperson, who follows the rites and prayers designated for a lay minister.

## A. ORDER OF BLESSING

### INTRODUCTORY RITES

282    When the community has gathered, a suitable song may be sung. The minister says:

**In the name of the Father, and of the Son, and of the Holy Spirit.**

All make the sign of the cross and reply:

**Amen.**

283    A minister who is a priest or deacon greets those present in the following or other suitable words, taken mainly from sacred Scripture.

**May the Father of mercies, the God of all consolation, be with you all.**

And all reply:

**And also with you.**

---

284    A lay minister greets those present in the following words:

**Let us praise the Father of mercies, the God of all consolation. Blessed be God for ever.**

**R. Blessed be God for ever.**

---

285    In the following or similar words, the minister prepares those present for the blessing.

**For those who trust in God,**
**in the pain of sorrow there is consolation,**
**in the face of despair there is hope,**
**in the midst of death there is life.**
**N. and N., as we mourn the death of your child we place ourselves in the hands of God and ask for strength, for healing, and for love.**

# READING OF THE WORD OF GOD

186 A reader, another person present, or the minister reads a text of sacred Scripture.

**Brothers and sisters, listen to the words of the book of Lamentations:**    3:17-26

*Hope in the Lord.*

**My soul is deprived of peace,**
**I have forgotten what happiness is;**
**I tell myself my future is lost,**
**all that I hoped for from the Lord.**
**The thought of my homeless poverty**
**is wormwood and gall;**
**Remembering it over and over**
**leaves my soul downcast within me.**
**But I will call this to mind,**
**as my reason to have hope:**
**The favors of the LORD are not exhausted,**
**his mercies are not spent;**
**They are renewed each morning,**
**so great is his faithfulness.**
**My portion is the LORD, says my soul;**
**therefore will I hope in him.**
**Good is the LORD to one who waits for him,**
**to the soul that seeks him;**
**It is good to hope in silence**
**for the saving help of the LORD.**

287    Or:

Isaiah 49:8-13—*In a time of favor I answer you, on the day of salvation I help you.*

Romans 8:18-27—*In hope we were saved.*

Romans 8:26-31—*If God is for us, who can be against us?*

Colossians 1:9-12—*We have been praying for you unceasingly.*

Hebrews 5:7-10—*Christ intercedes for us.*

Luke 22:39-46—*Agony in the garden.*

288    As circumstances suggest, one of the
following responsorial psalms may be sung, or
some other suitable song.

**R. To you, O Lord, I lift up my soul.**

Psalm 25

**Your ways, O LORD, make known to me;
teach me your paths,
Guide me in your truth and teach me,
for you are God my savior,
and for you I wait all the day.   R.**

**Remember that your compassion, O LORD,
and your kindness are from of old.
The sins of my youth and my frailties remember not;
in your kindness remember me
because of your goodness, O LORD.   R.**

**Look toward me, and have pity on me,
for I am alone and afflicted.
Relieve the troubles of my heart,
and bring me out of my distress.   R.**

**Preserve my life, and rescue me;
let me not be put to shame, for I take refuge
in you.
Let integrity and uprightness preserve me,
because I wait for you, O LORD.   R.**

Psalm 143:1, 5-6, 8, 10

**R. (v.1) O Lord, hear my prayer.**

289    As circumstances suggest, the minister
may give those present a brief explanation of
the biblical text, so that they may understand
through faith the meaning of the celebration.

71

# INTERCESSIONS

290    The intercessions are then said. The minister introduces them and an assisting minister or one of those present announces the intentions. From the following those best suited to the occasion may be used or adapted, or other intentions that apply to the particular circumstances may be composed.

The minister:

**Let us pray to God who throughout the ages has heard the cries of parents.**

**R. Lord, hear our prayer.**

Assisting minister:

**For N. and N., who know the pain of grief, that they may be comforted, we pray. R.**

Assisting minister:

**For this family, that it may find new hope in the midst of suffering, we pray. R.**

Assisting minister:

**For these parents, that they may learn from the example of Mary, who grieved by the cross of her Son, we pray. R.**

Assisting minister:

**For all who have suffered the loss of a child, that Christ may be their support, we pray. R.**

291    After the intercessions the minister, in the following or similar words, invites all present to sing or say the Lord's Prayer.

**Let us pray to the God of consolation and hope, as Christ has taught us:**

All:

**Our Father . . .**

## PRAYER OF BLESSING

292    A minister who is a priest or deacon says the prayer of blessing with hands out-stretched over the parents; a lay minister says the prayer with hands joined.

**Compassionate God,**
**soothe the hearts of N. and N.,**
**and grant that through the prayers of Mary,**
**who grieved by the cross of her Son,**
**you may enlighten their faith,**
**give hope to their hearts,**
**and peace to their lives.**

**Lord,**
**grant mercy to all the members of this family**
**and comfort them with the hope**
**that one day we will all live with you,**
**with your Son Jesus Christ, and the Holy**
    **Spirit,**
**for ever and ever.**

**R. Amen.**

293    Or:

**Lord,**
**God of all creation**
**we bless and thank you for your tender care.**
**Receive this life you created in love**
**and comfort your faithful people in their**
    **time of loss**
**with the assurance of your unfailing mercy.**

**We ask this through Christ our Lord.**

**R. Amen.**

As circumstances suggest, the minister in silence may sprinkle the parents with holy water.

294     A minister who is a priest or deacon concludes the rite by saying:

**May God be with you in your sorrow,
and give you light and peace.**

**R. Amen.**

**May God raise you up from your grief.**

**R. Amen.**

**May God grant you encouragement and
strength to accept his will.**

**R. Amen.**

Then he blesses all present.

**And may almighty God bless you all,
the Father, and the Son, and the
Holy Spirit.**

**R. Amen.**

---

295     A lay minister concludes the rite by signing himself or herself with the sign of the cross and saying:

**May God give us peace in our sorrow,
consolation in our grief,
and strength to accept his will in all things.**

**R. Amen.**

---

196     It is preferable to end the celebration with a suitable song.